by Philip Whalen
1961

Big Bridge Press

(C) Philip Whalen 1961

Editor: Michael Rothenberg
Illustrations: Philip Whalen
Cover and book design: Bradley Miskell
Cover Photograph: Walter Lehrman

With many thanks to Walter Lehrman for permission to reprint his
photograph of Philip Whalen and Jack Kerouac.

ISBN: 1-878471-07-4

Big Bridge Press
2000 Highway 1
Pacifica, CA 94044

650/355-4857

www.bigbridge.org
e-mail: walterblue@bigbridge.org

EDITOR'S NOTE

Michael: I am getting ready to publish Goofbook. Is there anything you want me to add or say?

Philip: This is a private letter that fell into the wrong hands. It should never be published. But if you have to do it then that's that.

Michael: I hate to think of myself as the wrong hands.

Philip: I was speaking metaphysically.

Philip Whalen and Jack Kerouac were friends.

May 4, 2001
San Francisco

GOOFBOOK

for Jack Kerouac

A book, for Jack, saying whatever I want to say, whatever I feel like saying (I just stepped on a tack-- luckily it was lying on edge-- in my sock feet & swore "God fuck us all!") a pretty bouquet of parsnips for Lord Mountjoy herald to the King as any I know or hope to meet. But now Rick & Les are shouting from one end of the house to the other about some professor Rick saw in Vesuvio's for the first time in 10,000 years, since Rick was a student at Berkeley, that is.

Under water, & a drip through my skylight, rag in the bottom of mountain cookpot silences Rain.

I lie in sleepingbag writing on clipboard arm/shoulder crease fine hairs, naked in feather sack.

Say when. Now. Bother. All other "my brother", Jack writes in front of book he gives to me…now he alone, Northport attic working music reading sleep room, Mémère & kitties asleep downstairs.

Amenhotep pterodactyl (wing fingers) Egyptian mill-moth meandering downy Nile woven-bottom boat to Happy Land Shakespeare says, "O Bottom, thou art translated" onager head, SET (the hot wind rocking the soul-boat off its Osiris course) gators in the cane-brakes hollering for Al Jolson white gloves mushmouth tear-smeared grin.

You don't expect to get away with that, she says, like she controlled every possible vibratory nuance of the scene I says I don't

1

know what you think I'm trying & I don't care & walked out & left her flat. She comes crying around to Minnie next day about unreasonable bastards why do I always have to pay why do I always have to go through all this every time.

TOTAL LOSS, Kenneth keeps hollering about "emotional bankruptcy" like Edmund Wilson talking about Fitzgerald.

Never trust a fountain pen; always use a pencil.
Fake topaze lying on my floor, emblem of chastity.
How come we need somebody so much we can't stand having them around? Both of us have this problem. "Fragments", Duncan named his book, "Of A Disordered Devotion". Well, at least he knows he's hung on his own head, his warped eyeballs, I say a great man-- what do you think of that? There. & now I'm tired & want to sleep & want also to go on writing this. "Habit", you always say (& right) "like benny pill-head", & drags me, disorganized blah, I got to see or feel a pattern a point an end...contrariwise if I see the end I stop before I get there because it ain't interesting if I can already see it. If I want to draw picture of a hand I put one down flat on the paper & push the pencil around it, why bother?

I know I can stand up & walk out of this room. Lots of other things that I'm not doing. Do I secretly know that I'm doing this the way I want to do it? Shall I continue? Of course. But now I feel dumb & self-conscious about it. hung-up, blah, blooie & fooie. At Woey Loey Goey restaurant they still got those hot greasy pork rolls, Chinese you remember the all-night underground corner of Grant & Jackson San Francisco

2

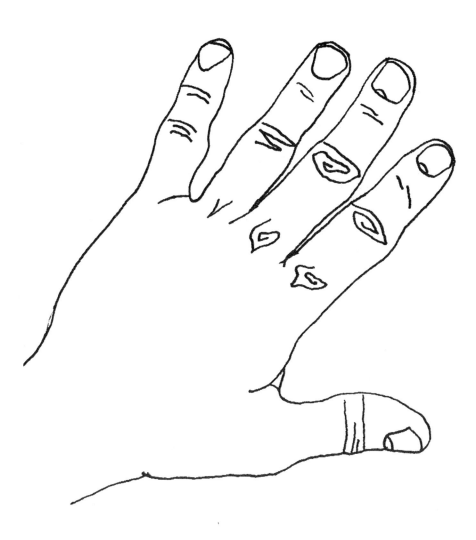

IT FALLS

carelessly, into a stream of consciousness, which is the mistake the
stream of memory &c. NOT INTERESTING WHAT'S WANTED IS
UNCONSCIOUS STREAM OF PLEASURE, COME, PEE, ETC. If my
dick was hard I'd trace it on the paper here but instead will fake it.

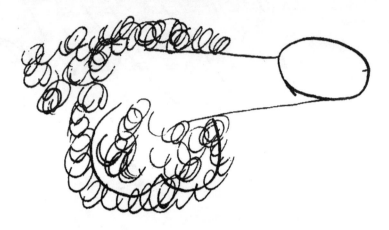

which is really what goes right there in any (& every, while I am this
particular temporary collection of temporary/changing molecules)
case; ideas/habits/history-- springing beyond it via irrational mind
possibility: invention, poem, insanity, vision <u>samadhi</u> drug high, booze
high, natural euphoria or hard-on of the brain-- the unexpected last
minute twist or loop that defeats Marx, Freud, cops, etc. The man
said "PLUS CA CHANGE" &C., the more it changes the samer it gets
(but was right only about politics, he was talking about the French
Revolution & after) what we know is

CUNT

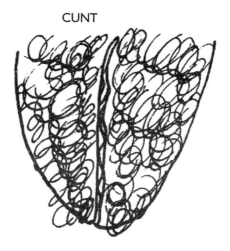

which is always different, the real answer to whatever question intellectual or otherwise.

Thinking now of returning to first pages of this & taking out quotes of Shakespeare, Egypt, Duncan-- but I'm supposed to say what I want: why censor what I know-- Osiris, for example-- any more than I should stop myself from writing FUCK or other "improper" words?

Brilliant clear day now, trying to continue this for you, & worrying about money which hasn't been mailed to me yet for last Connecticut reading. I wanted to buy three volumes of Arthur Avalon (Sir John Woodroffe) on Tantric philosophy. Oh well, Monday...? (although Les would loan me money to do it today I hate to ask him, & also fear getting hung up with reading the books instead of writing this-- & now he's just come in here, bright storefront living-room where I write & asks

"Any mail?"

"No, not today. It's already been delivered all up & down the street... I've been out already, mailing letters."

"Do you want to go to the bookstore?", combing his hair down over his forehead & glasses before parting it

"Yes."

"OK, soon as I get a cup of coffee.")

No problems. Sunshine & clear air after the flood slop last night. But continue, while waiting, no idea what comes next.

Apples. For you. O, & I was thinking how the world looks different, when you see, understand, know that luck, that life is changed, different, that something bad can happen suddenly, bringing on further change as easily as a lucky break-- but conscious of an end to it: actually everything good has happened, & everything bad-- & can I go on from here, from whatever top or bottom this is I've reached. Necessity now to invent, to change into something else, change myself

***

What I did was sit still & then I traveled. I was silent & then I spoke. People asked me questions & I answered them. Then I returned home. A complete lifetime came & went. A world appeared, flourished-- laughing & crying, pain & delight, beauty & ugliness-- & slowly dissolved away. Now I rest, awake, thinking of its history, recording. Free also not to do this. I could go out & pick flowers, go to sleep, rob the bank down the street-- EVERYTHING CAN BE DONE!

A while ago, I sat in formal meditation, because that was what had, then, to happen-- next, wash the defrosted refrigerator, wash the dishes, drink some coffee & smoke while writing this: which must be done right now, this way:

I don't know if these are hydrangea or ginger blossoms-- flowers appearing from the pencil & leaves: EVERYTHING IS POSSIBLE, EVERYTHING IS IMPOSSIBLE

some sort of goofy water-bird going towards a pond, QUACK or HONK, grackle, etc.

When it's warm enough in here (I've lighted the gas oven, our only heat)-- I'll take a shower, I enjoy washing & inspecting my body, my skin is very fine.

The thing is, I've just discovered, I'm not WRITING much of this, I'm putting down what I think or see or hear inside & outside my head-- the pencil is writing & I am, I guess, elsewhere, or feeling/thinking something which doesn't show here, isn't yet broke through onto the page-- except maybe in the case of those flowers, ducks &c. above. Question mark. I keep forgetting that this is paper & graphite-- the "modern" painters from Cezanne to Picasso have complained that the academic & historical painters were trying to make the viewer forget that he was looking at something made of canvas & paint, tried to make the audience imagine it was looking at real persons or seeing out of a window. Maybe I think the reader as he looks at this is looking at me instead of words? "A fearful error, my dear!", as Burroughs says,

So, I shall write a word.
              (& immediately, I'm stuck, can't think of a word-- but suppose I put down one that I like) .... (long pause to think)
              PECULIAR
& I suppose I could arrange a whole lot of such words into pieces like Stein's TENDER BUTTONS, but that isn't what I want to do, seeing that it is possible & already been done. Likewise, telling a story is out of the question, I can tell a story in a couple of pages & get bored with it. (I don't throw it away afterwards, I keep everything I write, but there it stays & I forget it.) & poems are a nuisance, I write lots of

them, some people like them but the poems seldom tell all I must--
only what must be written right then.

Same with book for you. I think, "where will it go from here"--
& "isn't this the end of it?" & "9 pages of handwriting, a great deal of
space taken up with pictures, quotes & pompous essay isn't a book" &
I am resolved (I tell myself) not to stop until I come to the end of
"words I want to put here."

Doing this & WRITING-- same difference as between
indiscriminate balling, jacking off & c., & fucking with a woman you
love & who loves you in return. One is momentary pleasure; the
other is making it, a high, a breakthrough.

<pre>
    MORE   MORNING   A TURNING
                    VISION
                        NOT ocular,
knowledge/feeling/instant: THIS IS THE WAY IT IS
            TATHATA ("SUCH")
                as music, what it is
(I guess) when you're digging Sinatra
      TOTAL POSSIBILITY FREEDOM SHAPE WORLDS NOW YES
                            all kinds worlds
happening happy all directions-- also gone by & nothing changed nor
even started
                    OK
                in any case
I'm fond of saying
                "A RARE DELIGHT"
</pre>

Like all the people I love I think you suffer too much or anyhow more than necessary & in that aspect you're a meathead-- while realizing that you're very great-- in fact almost anybody is got more on the ball, more brains, compassion &c. than I

                        *

        & now I stop & cook dinner
                        *
        & wait for it to bake
                        *

PRAJNAPARAMITAHRIDAYA MANTRAM: GATE, GATE, PARAGATE, PARASAMGATE, BODHI, SVAHA!
                        i.e.:
"Dinner will be ready sometime. Mitloaf, baked acorn squash, spuds, salad, new pot of coffee, cheese & fruit. SVAHA!" Thitherwards my heart is yearning. Also my belly. Even so, the BRIDARANYAKA UPANISHAD says, "Breath to air & to the immortal! Then this my body ends in ashes. OM! Mind, Remember! Remember thy deeds! Mind, Remember! Remember thy deeds!"
        (5th Adhyaya, 15th Brahmana, 3)

Meatloaf crackles in the oven.

        TORN IRON, which reminds me, say hello from me to Larry Rivers.

                        EXTRA
                        Depend on it, everything comes,
for example those 3 volumes of Sir John Woodroffe--   but will go again, sure as God make little green apples.

Words have nothing to do with it & yet are as much, as SUCH, as anything else, they also play

scratching the tip of my nose

CANDELABRA, I like THAT word, fancy candlesticks, glass, silver, porcelain, wood, brass, on the church altar or dinner-table, &c. See what I mean? & have lighted the way! I was surprised at United Nations lobby (Allen took me there just before I caught my jet home) at one end a bad green plaster copy of big Zeus statue (GIFT OF GREECE) & at the other, a Foucault pendulum suspended from the ceiling (1/4 mile up, it looks like) swinging, proving to all comers that the Earth turns under our feet. The meaning of this juxtaposition of emblemata, ikons, ideas.... Holy Toledo! Whuz going on?

****

Yesterday I goofed, reading-- no meditation, no writing, Now's the last day of this month, end of November & new beginning of this extravaganza

Big pinecone on the table, gift of John Montgomery, of proper size & weight to build a thyrsus

IO! EVOI!

as carried by Greek ladies running mad over the mountains, now they trot goggle-eyed from Magnins to the City of Paris to Ransohoff's grabbing a fur here a scarf there a jewel, fragments of the lost torn scattered body of Osiris, & always the wrong piece, never the long dong they really need to satisfy & comfort them, although the stores are full & newly decorated with christmas goodies of every description, ----

THAT STAR, THAT 5-POINT STAR

enclosing, as Leonardo (or somebody) calculated

MAN, (in proportion, of course, had it all figured out mathematically)

STAR

& woman also, but her light a different range of vibration a different part of the spectrum, a different frequency. Man's eye sees no light

beyond RED ORANGE YELLOW GREEN BLUE VIOLET, with his
eyes, but feels senses her being where he sees only darkness, a
cloud-- from which the star is presently revealed, THE MYSTERY OF
THE INCARNATION which is as we say Christmas, the CHILD
appears in the midst of the congregation, the priest carries him
singing to the crêche in the chapel on the gospel side of the High
Altar singing & we are PRESENT in the flesh, light from one star...

all this is pretty fancy, coming from one dried pinecone-- squirrels &
mice are asleep on top of seedpile they got from it, holes & burrows
high in the Sierra now under 10 or 15 feet of snow & more to come,
considering that it's raining here in San Francisco & I see a seagull out
the window, probably another storm coming in from the sea (also
dark/light, STELLA MARIS) I hear sparrows

& remember Mt Hozomeen as seen from Sourdough Mtn. or
Desolation Peak-- the trident of Siva whose shakti is Uma, daughter
of Himalaya-- as well as my initial in the sky, -- W-- my mountain?

Look out my store window, Twin Peaks green November rain. When I set out for the east last month they were motionless dry hills or alive only at night in moon stars a fine line-- now awake ALL the time-- & maybe all this blah I'm putting down here will also grow-- a superstitious hope-- walk in the rain myself & turn my brains all green? But the world & me is Maya, whatever color... magic love play picture in the day/night.

OH OH OH OH

ARCHES & PILLARS, windows across the street, a cushion unpropped from the wall falls on my feet kids & cars hollering outside the arrested rain

What would Dostoievsky make out of all this? I being some dopey old crap like Verhovensky in THE POSSESSED: indolent, genteel, full of goofy notions, occasionally excited, gradually building up a mass of torment.

But that's more fancy literary twaddle, I want NOW, NEW, Let me repeat:

TWIN PEAKS GREEN

NOVEMBER

RAIN

Mind wandering, but not really making the scene, projecting it

HERE

EGGPLANT

shiny purple, a beautiful shape

Doughnut pistol! Phonograph porridge! (Imitation Gregory speech) The bus went past just now & took my mind with it; I was going to say something very important.

(Lawyer's joke:

"I deny the allegations & I defy the alligator!")

DREARY, & yet OK, so it ain't noble as if I lay down on the page & set fire to my hair hollering: Pelican soap! Mycenaean rocks of morning dance in gold Achilles tomb, Death goat hooves of thrashing net my weepy ears, my beauty wish-- yet will I varnish ivory hero smoke! Unfreeze Andromeda from the drunken stoneflash seas, etc.

I don't mean to put Gregory down, I only wish I could do it as wild, project as much energy, invent so wide & so well.

WORRIED FISH

I got this here now breast of lamb mess in the oven, stewing away in onions, celery, olive oil, rum, sherry, bitters, lemon juice, herbs, GARLIC & a shot of sugar to put a bowknot on top. I'll put in the other vegetables later. It will be delicious.

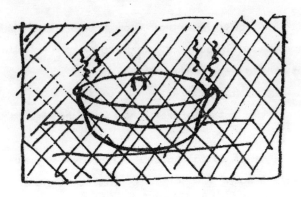

dark hot blackness in the oven...
the fumes are unbelievable! Delicate scents, aromas &c.

Spark tangle, the stars among which we move, in hatefulness & all
delight, bubbling putrefaction in $10,000 bronze casket, decay itself
luminescent, the dear bone-box excavated later archeological curio-
sity museum or filled with geraniums, rich man's estate gardens,
"A charming conceit"-- (carved Roman sarcophaguses now hold stu-
dent umbrellas-- lobby of USC Library) -- ONE IS ONE, the old song
says, AND ALL ALONE/AND EVERMORE/SHALL BE SO.

AMONG STARS IN THE MOTHER'S LAP ("'S Lids!", folks used to
swear, meaning "By God's Eyelids!") here we go from potty to Vatican
to bawdy house to bank to gaol to loonybin, merry & bright, a little
murder here, a little mayhem there, here a fuck, there a cocksuck,
everywhere a saint a monster a beautiful wife & family eternal war
eternal symphony eternal Bach B MINOR MASS eternal soap-bubble
rainbow palace love & art & compassion & wisdom & enlightenment

& hello & there you are, here we were, beautiful stew in the oven

tears.... mud....orchid....cancer

NOTHING IS POSSIBLE

EVERYTHING IS IMPOSSIBLE

MIRACLE VISION BRAT

("Eat your dinner, Brat!", Peter tells you)

"CRABMEAT LULLABY FOR DINNER AGAIN?!"

BEAUTIFUL EGGPLANTS

(Aubergines)

got seeds like tomatoes

& OPIUM CANDY for dessert

a dipperful

WHAT IS. In any direction, life & death. (By the way, a visit to the Boston Museum of Fine Arts taught me that I had been misled-- the figure of Siva Nataraja ((Siva, Lord of the Dance)) has all 3 eyes OPEN, not in the least sleepy.)

WHAT IS.

One of the stations on the old interurban line Portland to Oregon City was called Bellflower. That was then.

Bellflower, Campanula, a fairly intense blue, much farther back than Portland, years before-- back in The Dalles: campanula, snapdragon, sweetwilliam, lilac, tulip, iris, & nasturtium: RED YELLOW & BLUE those flowers I still love, true color, are sometimes here, that will be when. See what I mean?

but you have turned your head away, to Lowell, to your own child river, Thoreau's Merrimac. My river, the Columbia, still unknown-- except to three men I knew in college who traveled the whole length of it, Canada glacier swamp to Astoria Pacific mouth, canoe & sleepingbags a little grub & spare pair of sox apiece--HAVE IT while I've got

18

                              naked summer night swim I float
past our shore fire into the dark face up air water stars limitless
day/night ALL CONTINUUM ALIVE a loss of me
                         PANIC
I swim back to the fire. Some river.

My mother & father in sportboat with friends nearly drowned in giant
storm waves near Crates Point West of The Dalles where the
Columbia Gorge begins, the river nearly a mile wide there. The
Merrimac reminds me of the Willamette (which has spring floods like
yours) generally calm & gentle winding river-- Constable,
Gainsborough trees along the banks....

                      HOPELESS NOW
(as I floated then, senseless in star water) to

        PUT   WORD   HERE

it (word) gets hung up in memory, "experience", description, expres-
sion

        IT WAS MY HEAD THAT TURNED AWAY

& fucks everything up, I'm terrified (I suppose) of SPEAKING, afraid
to believe, to realize that I can't write, don't want to write or say any-
thing-- & perversely, here it appears, WHAT IS, a scramble, a grubbage
pile-- actually quite wonderful... if anything were total in this partial
shifting world, I could truly say I AM TOTALLY SELF-DECEIVED

                                                        19

Howsomever in the process of change-your-partners-&-turn-about, I'm totally whoopee for an age or two, & so on.... zum to zeedle to framp. HO! Which is to say there ain't no mystery to it.

THERE

as the Tibetans say, considerable difference from pornographic fantasy, & I said in my poem, "It don't mean what it looks like & the description misleads."

WHAT IS, all the pairs of opposites at once, BOTH/AND, mama &
papa night & day, knowing & doing, life & death-- you say, "Nothing
ever happened anyway-- everything is all right"-- & I must reply,
"Everything has happened, is happening, will happen: all right, all
wrong, all good & all evil-- but only temporarily, only as we are in the
habit of seeing it-- what's happening is what we NAME nothing, shun-
yata &c. (giving a name to _____ a state beyond description the
suchness, TATHATA, etc.) NOTHING IS HAPPENING LIKE CRAZY
ALL OVER 10,000 worlds (including, yes, THIS, which has been stand-
ing still while I've been stirring the stew)

    NO   NO   NO   NO   NO   NO   NO

I don't want to lay out all this argument, windy honk noise, all the
wrong words books full of them for centuries we ourselves must be
walking law wheels try every known & unknown way to become
great beings, liberators-- KNOWING that there is nothing to be lib-
erated, that it's been done already, only I caught in life & death trap

MOVE ON!

& promptly move into middle of H-bomb in process of fusion or some-
thing equally messy, head into a meatgrinder &c.

23-- SKIDOO!

I always believe anything you tell me because sooner or later it turns
our you were right; however, during the interim, I tend to drag my feet.

Turtle approaching chrysanthemums as they speed

past.

WHAT IS.

I have no patience; I give up too easy. If I haven't accomplished 10 years' work between the time I get up in the morning & bedtime, I scream at myself that I'm no good, I shall never do anything, &c. How can I write one word at a time, even one page a day? I must produce a 1000-page book in any period of waking! & neither knowledge nor means of manufacturing word #1.

LOOK.

Raining again, I hope not enough to start the skylight leak routine.

THUMB
FUR ANIMAL
SLEEK SWURGE UNDERWATER
SEA (LION?) SEA-OTTER!
LIES BACK ON SWELL, KELP FOOD
INNOCENT WATCHFUL EYE

Which puts us a couple of months ago at Slate's Hotsprings, 5 poets boiling in egg-water 8 feet above ocean slurp below sun breeze washing over skin like finest oil-- a secret history-- how could 5 such animals all the same shape accomplish such a variety of work, repre- sent so many different worlds-- completely visible to each other yet so distinctly private, separate, unique? Empedocles says "wander each alone beside life's sea" ... & secretly, I guess, at war with each other-- No wonder Wolfe cried out

O, LOST!

warring for that same bright Helen or Mama, the truce only tempo-
rary, some other poet hollers even more concisely,

"O MY ENEMY, MY BROTHER!"

In some sense or other I suppose Robert Graves is right-- the Muse
chooses a man & then connives with his alter ego to do away with
him, the new lover enjoys his season & is in his turn cut down. But I
get more sense out of Wm Carlos Williams' version-- "Turn the cities
& all their conveniences over to the women & the kids-- throw the
men out into the countryside to farm & hunt & fight to kill off the
weak ones-- let them back into town once a year to breed & then
throw them out again. Everything would be healthier." (This is some-
thing he said to us years ago; I don't know that he wrote it anywhere.)

All that's memory & history again but in a funny way all of us are
somehow closer to history, making up a lot of it as we go along-- ten
years ago I wouldn't have imagined myself zooming back & forth
across the country in airplane delivering the dharma in person coast-
to-coast-- what would Coleridge think of that? (Mila Repa didn't need
a flying machine, though-- I don't really boast-- & notion that dharma
needs delivering is only personal delusion, the wheel turns whether I
say aye, yes or no anyway)

TOOTHACHE MISERY stops me here. Still I want
to get ahead of history just a little anyway, disentangle at least one
foot, or my writing hand, to be free of it & be now

WHAT IS

MOVE ON, discover &/or
invent something else several other worlds freer, less hung up than

this one has been. & I, yes, I want to (of course) say "Look, Ma, looka ME, hey, Ma, looka what I'M doing, looky, Ma, LOOK!" Why not? That's there as much as the freckles on my face. I accept that. But worse than my freckles, pride, egoism, madness, are my cupidity, ignorance & attachment-- all these to be altered converted into bodhi--

       & MOVE ON

                It's raining so hard that I'm damn sure my roof is leaking, & here comes Les shouting "God's-a-pity, Man, the rain is coming through & your mattress is awash & floating about the room, you took that pot away!" He's re-reading all the Elizabethans again, so his speech is grown extravagant. I put mountain cookpot with rag in bottom, first wiping up small puddle & splash, under leak-- bed not really wet, this was jovial exaggeration on L.'s part, but

       I MOVED
& the world is saved from drowning-- temporarily.

Now 3 A.M. & tired toothache & elbow tired of holding me up (clip-board on livingroom couch) & so to bed again the waves & feathers, Vishnu asleep on feather serpent Kukulcan

         O, BOOK!   be still too, shut up your yakking & silly dramatizing & fogging & sleep: NO MORE WORDS!

    & no more stars, rain all night, backporch & bathroom flooded, more leaks in my skylight than pots to catch drips-- After breakfast feeble sun in & out of clouds-- & start of Enlightenment Festival week, December 1-8 it was on the 8th Gautama was completely enlightened under the koolibah tree & so all must meditate every day this week & 24 hours beginning on the 7th-- sunrise on the 8th all monks & layfolks &c. are supposed to have made our own Nirvana or at least to have tried with might & main. (N.B., that Advent is celebrated by the Church on or about that date, 4 Sundays before Xmas)

DULLNESS
I watch the heatwaves whibbling up from the kerosene heater
NO MAIL TODAY

perhaps my horoscope is all bitched up
somebody mis-handled the Tarot deck, put the I-CHING away upside
down, "joggled" (an obscure Author says) "the Al-Mu-Kan-Tar"
HI-DE-HO.
Anything (of course!) outside, anything except my own goofiness is
(surely) responsible for my present state.....
GOOFBOOK
Bottlecrash, the Canada Dry delivery truck loads bubbly into corner
Chinese store
ON THE WALLS, maps of the John Muir Trail &
High Sierra Region, big portrait of my mug by Mike McClure, & on
this side, what looks like beautiful abstract painting but is colored &
shaded relief map of Yosemite Valley-- all the rest is white paint.
GOOFBOOK, laugh & cry, look at the ceiling, out the window,
rearrange & tenderly scratch your balls.

Leslie says "Where is my mail? Why are you hiding all my let-
ters?" & I tell him I'm gathering them up & tying with red satin bow
to give him for Christmas present. "You are, too", he says, "Some
Christmas present! What's the news out there? Who won the Trojan
War?" (He's still abed) I say "Everybody lost"-- which is the truth &
all this is happening. In a way, I prefer it to writing a novel although
I'll try that, too, I suppose, as well as everything else. Meanwhiles, this
is the 30th (holograph) page of GOOF & all the paper I happen to
have on my clipboard so this is all you get until I start typing it up
which may add more of everything, pictures, sobs, leaks, polemics,
--PACHYDERMS!.

28

Where would the world be without HIPPO, ELEPHANT, RHINO?
Without some notion of huge gentle patience giant love lazily wan-
dering rivers & woods wherever its pleasure leads, nothing to stand in
its way

Me, I grope & stumble, forgetting their example but have man-
aged to get this far with Sri Ganesa's help (elephant-headed son of
Siva; remover of obstacles, broke off his tusk to write with, patron of
letters whose yana is a rat what can gnaw his way through anything)

SRI-GANESAYA NAMAH!, the Indians say,
HOMAGE TO LORD GANESA!

END OF GOOFBOOK FOR JACK